# Demon to Dinner

## Journeying Towards a Greater Self-Love

Jason Miller

# CONTENTS

# Acknowledgments

I could not have done this without the constant guidance from Inspiration and Intuition. Thank you to Spirit, who I leaned on to guide me through this journey without losing myself. Life, Universe, Source, Spirit, Gurus: you all helped me awaken to my higher Self. Because of you, I tapped back into true and lasting peace, joy and love.

Thank you to poet A. Love for allowing her poems to be a part of making this book magical!

# Note from the Author

There are parts of our core-being, either surfaced or in the deep edges, that I like to call our "perceived inner demons." They are a part of who we are or show up in our lives in some shape or form. They are often perceived as the "ugly" parts of us, yet our relationship with them can shift depending on our intention.

**Demons can come in a variety of forms: chronic anxiety, chronic depression, obsessive compulsive disorder, limiting beliefs, the wounded inner child, negative thoughts, self-worth deficits, vices, addictions, self-hate mindset, regrets, negative body image, anger, fear, guilt, hurt, effects of traumas, etc. It can come from being different from the perceived "norm": sexual identity, gender identity, distinct personality traits, a disability. Demons can also come from internalized experiences of the past that are stuck within the body/mind/emotions.**

Some demons, including disorders, traumas, and diseases, require expertise. This journey is one that I went through allowing me to loosen the bounds weighing on me so I could truly touch the Light within. This process is not a treatment or cure for any perceived demon; instead, it is a map for shifting one's relationship with any demon: why fight it when you can invite it to dinner?

As one of my favorite spiritual teachers, Mooji, states, "Personal growth comes when we learn to fully accept ourselves with where we are at." It is then that we can observe the situation without identifying with the demon or label. And from that space, we can choose how we will continue on. Some people choose to run from their demons most of their lives. It is crucial to remember that our demons are the greatest teachers. Mooji often states, "What you're looking FOR is exactly what you're looking FROM."

Your world is a projection and mirror of yourself as a compass to awaken your higher Self. Accept the challenge. Tell the demon(s) to throw their best punch because you refuse to give into the illusion and become a symptom of delusion; you refuse to miss the Truth of who you are; you refuse to miss the lesson and gifts that come from meeting your demons face-to-face. We only have one appointment with Life: do not miss it.

Your demons show up for you, so show up for your demons. Be vulnerable and venturous enough to show up to dinner.

We are all doing the best we know how to do with the resources we have, and we all have resources at our disposal. Grab hold and use them because this journey shakes the very fibers of the inner being. And remember, be gentle, patient and kind with yourself during this journey.

Some of the resources I have used along my journey include prayer, meditation, yoga, gurus and teachers, recreational activities in nature, travel, reading, my surrounding community, Reiki, chiropractic, EFT, NLP, worship services of many traditions, Quantum Connect, Access Consciousness, forgiveness processes, Emotion/Body code, Mental Emotional Release, etc.).

There is no destination to reach, only the journey that reveals the True Self.

# Prologue

## The Love U Give

The golden rule is a universal human code: treat others as you would like to be treated; in other words, love your neighbor as yourself.

The irony is that we usually treat ourselves worse than others through thoughts, words and actions. The love you give yourself is too often deficient.

Before you can live the golden rule or love another as yourself, you must learn to be with the love you give yourself. It must start with you.

That means loving ALL of you: the unexplored dark, ugly parts of you as well. And that is where the journey to transformation truly begins.

What makes us who we are is the duality that exists: the inner beauty and the inner ugly, the light and the dark, the good and the bad. We were born to shine our light, and ironically, in order to do that, we must face our inner demons. Not ignore them. Not suppress them. We must meet them, greet them, take notes from them, and calibrate our approach and relationship with them. We must lean in and face them.

You are whole. You are not broken. You were created with every trait, talent, gift, demon, weakness and strength required of you to fulfill your purpose and make a difference in this world. You were created with everything needed to truly release the potency of your existence.

Allow me to take you through my journey as we venture into the darkest crevices and caves I have ever dared to enter within myself to face the perceived inner demon I never wanted to face. It was in coming face-to-face with this demon that changed my life! My experiences and journey allowed me to truly understand the power of self-acceptance, congruency and love.

Alongside my story, I provide deeper insights (deep dives) to each phase in which I found myself. Then I offer magic questions to go even deeper and explore for yourself. Watch the magic happen as you explore these questions. There is power when you choose to live in the question. This book offers you the space to do just that as we go through each phase.

It is time to invite the demon to dinner. And as you do so, may you constantly be with *the love U give.*

# Introduction

One of my favorite stories is that of a monk who lives in a cave:

*One day, a monk leaves his cave to search for firewood. Upon his return, he finds that demons have taken over his cave. His initial reaction is to get rid of them. He exerts all of his energy, forcefully trying to get the demons out of his cave but fails at this attempt. The monk then decides to reason with the demons, but instead of leaving the cave, the demons begin mocking the monk. Finally, the monk surrenders and sits on the floor of this cave. He looks into each of the demon's eyes and says, "I'm not going anywhere and it looks like you're not either. If we are going to be here together, then please come and join me for tea. Teach me everything you have to offer." And at that moment the demons disappear.*

It is in times of surrendering to the lessons that our inner demons hold that we truly become liberated and transformed. It is the most difficult task to take on, and one that takes courage, but it is worth the journey.

There is a teaching that has proven true throughout my life: the cause of all suffering comes from either trying to hold onto something or push it away. No one can hold onto someone or something forever; life is impermanent. Also, if we become attached to something, someone or an expectation, it will ultimately lead us into suffering because we are attached to how it shows up in our reality instead of just allowing it to be. On the flip side, the more we try to suppress or avoid something, the more it appears, sometimes even more intensely than before. Resisting life and becoming attached to this reality always result in some form of suffering.

This is a journey of allowance and acceptance to lead to our best selves!

## *Demon to Dinner*

*Why does a person spend so much time trying on everything,
except themselves?*

*Hiding behind everything that isn't them to find a place in their
world.*

*Evil. Good. Hate. Love. Violence. Peace. Poison. Cleansing.*

*Every human being has dark, ugly swirled into their light, beauty.*

*Try to destroy the inner demon
Hold on. Resist. Avoid.
It becomes powerful!*

*Looking deeper, a new light burns.*

*What if we instead invite the inner demon to dinner?
"Welcome, teach me everything you have to offer."*

*As host, offer your guest a seat at the table.*

*One-on-one with your demon.
Vulnerability—no façade as refuge.
Raw. Open. Trusting.*

*Radical Acceptance. Gentle Approach. Love Abound.*

*Present Day*

Grams,

*"It's been a long day without you my friend, and I'll tell you all about it when I see you again."*

Even after five years, I still cannot get the image out of my head as I played this song repeatedly watching as you were lowered into the ground, never to hear your voice or feel your touch again.

I have so much to tell you, so much to share with you since you've been gone. I want you to know that I am currently doing the best I have ever been in my entire life. For the first time in my life, I feel fulfilled and truly authentic. For the first time, I can say that I am truly happy. I am living the life that I created and was born to live. I am always learning new things and continuing to get out of my comfort zone stretching myself to new horizons.

But I don't want to get ahead of myself. It has been five years since I last saw you, last heard your voice, last spoke to you.

I am writing this in hopes that it reaches you, somehow. You see, there was something I wanted to share with you, something I wanted to tell you. It was my biggest heartache, my heaviest secret, my scariest demon. I just couldn't find my way to tell you while I had you here.

*"Why'd you have to leave so soon? Why'd you have to go? Why'd you have to leave me when I needed you the most?"*

The echoes of the song still reverberate in my mind. Life sure is interesting in the journey She takes us through. You understand; you battled cancer the last few years of your life. And you were so valiant.

I wish I were as valiant as you were at the time. But fear paralyzed me. If I could go back in time and do it over, I would share even the heaviest parts of my heart with you.

# Phase I
# Awareness

*Five Years Prior*

Grams,

It was early one morning as I was waking up slowly. I received a *bing* on my phone. As I went to check it, I noticed it was from my fiancé at the time. You remember her--she spent that afternoon with you looking at wigs to cover your head during chemo. You loved trying on those wigs: a new personality revealed with each one. Anyways, I looked at the text message, and it read:

*I just woke up from a nightmare that you were gay and left me without even a care. I woke up extremely sad. Text me when you wake up!*

Immediately after reading that text, blood rushed to my face. I could feel my heartbeat pound within me. My breath quickened. I felt as if I had just been found out and caught in my secret that I didn't know I had and that I didn't give anyone permission to know. As I sat there, I realized that this was something I really had to look at: something that was real within me that I never allowed to be seen, heard or explored. Was I just insecure about my masculinity, comparing myself and envying what other men looked like or was there something more to it? Was I attracted to men?

This awareness scared me so much that I didn't allow myself to even think or say the word *gay or bisexual.* Only to ponder it in the back of my mind.

Grams, you know that I was always different from the typical guy. As a boy, I liked arts and crafts. I always wanted to tend to others and listen to what was on their mind and heart. I didn't love sports like most boys, but rather loved dancing, singing and music. I had more friends who were girls than who were boys. After elementary school, I can't really say I ever had a huge interest in girls like the average boy did. I remember being in middle school and high school trying to figure out where I fit in and who I was. I was friends with everyone; I didn't have my own exclusive group of friends. During that same time, I was trying on different versions of myself as most teenagers do and figuring out my masculinity. I found myself observing the way male peers acted and interacted and comparing myself to them. I remember wishing I could be as attractive or as muscular. I never felt like I belonged. I somewhat always figured that I was just balanced in my feminine and masculine qualities. But looking back now, I can see that there was more to it.

This morning's text message and my response fired an awareness that was loud enough for me to realize that it could not be ignored or suppressed.

# Deep Dive: Awareness

Awareness is crucial. Nothing changes in life without first becoming aware of it. The first step is always awareness of how something is the way it is.

All humans have both the beautiful and the ugly; the dark and the light; the demon and the angel; the bad and the good. The tendency is to focus on the parts of ourselves that are easiest to accept and either ignore or suppress the ugly parts of ourselves we do not love: we are usually harsh towards those parts of ourselves.

Perception is often filtered through distortion, deletion or generalization; it is often molded by family, community and society. It is crucial to put quotation marks around what we deem to be the "ugly" or "dark" sides of us. Our perceived demon(s) could just turn out to be our very best teacher(s) or friend(s).

In the phase of awareness, it is important to remain as neutral as possible: to just simply observe and be aware of what is, without identifying with *it*, without changing anything. It is helpful to come from a place of loving-kindness, compassion and mindfulness.

Becoming aware means simply noticing the situation and *the self* in the very moment without judgment and, as gently as possible, sensing and observing all edges, possibilities, and aspects of it and yourself.

# Magic Questions for Awareness

What makes me who I am?

What parts of me are easiest to love and accept?

What parts of me are most difficult to love and accept?

What are my demons?

What is the demon that wants my attention the most at this time of my life?

What aspects of me am I currently ignoring?

What are new edges of me that I have not become aware of until now?

What aspect of me am I currently trying to hide or avoid?

What am I holding onto most tightly in life?

Where do I hold the most fear, anger, sadness, guilt, hurt? Why?

What parts of my life make me miserable or are not as good as I know they could be?

Where am I playing small in life?

What makes me feel most joyful and the most fulfilled?

# Let the Magic Happen!
Journal Space for Personal Reflection

## SELF-AWARENESS

LOOK IN YOUR SOUL, BEAUTY IS DISCOVERED

BELIEVE IN YOURSELF, TALENTS ARE UNCOVERED

DIRECTIONS APPEAR, BY FOLLOWING YOUR HEART

UNDERSTAND INSIDE, YOU'RE CAPABLE AND SMART

SEAMLESSLY UNITE, YOUR INSPIRATION WITHIN

STRETCH YOUR DREAMS FURTHER, START TO BEGIN

LOVE YOUR REFLECTION, STARING INTO THE MIRROR

FORGIVE YOURSELF UNTIL, THE LESSONS ARE CLEAR

CONSTANTLY LEARN, THROUGH ALL THE MISTAKES

CONQUER YOUR FEARS, SEE PAST THE HEADACHES

THERE'S GOOD IN OTHERS, NO MATTER THE PAST

FIERCELY CLING TO HOPE, THE PAIN WON'T LAST

DOUBTS WILL APPEAR, SO LEAN ON YOUR FRIENDS

THEY'LL BUILD YOU UP, UNTIL YOUR HEART MENDS

EVERY DAY'S A CHOICE, UNDERSTAND YOUR DEAL

FIND HAPPINESS WITHIN, AND CONTINUE TO HEAL

STAY TRUE TO YOURSELF, AT THE END OF THE DAY

SELF AWARENESS IS, YOUR CONFIDENCE ON DISPLAY

A. LOVE

●

## LOOKING INTO MY SOUL

LOOKING INTO MY SOUL, DIFFERENT VERSIONS I WILL SEE

WHO IS THIS PERSON, AND HOW DID I COME TO BE

SOMEONE COMPLETELY DIFFERENT, BETTER THAN BEFORE

AFTER PICKING ALL THE PIECES, ONCE ON THE FLOOR

LEARNING LIFE'S LESSONS, SOMEWHAT THROWN AT ME

BUILDING UP MY STRENGTH, DODGING STONES I DIDN'T SEE

OTHERS I'LL SURROUND, BRINGING LOVE AND RESPECT

BURSTING THROUGH EXCITEMENT, HAPPINESS TO CONNECT

MY SURFACE WILL SHOW, WHAT I'VE CHOSEN TO ATTAIN

SEARCHING FOR PEACE, WITH A MOMENT TO EXPLAIN

A. LOVE

●

# Phase II
# Acknowledgment

Grams,

Do you remember when my fiancé and I ended the relationship after the weekend of our family reunion? Well, this new awareness within me wasn't the reason we broke off the engagement, but I have to say I was relieved. Something just felt off for both of us in different ways. It was best for both of us. It offered me the gift of space and time to really go deep within myself. The pain of the breakup was intense, yet the pain of losing you only weeks later took front stage in my heart.

Even though I now had this new awareness in my consciousness, I couldn't find a way to say or even think the words that defined this new inner demon. Hearing the words coming from my own mouth and entering into my ears felt impossible and unimaginable. With some time, I finally acknowledged my new awareness that, yes, I was attracted to men. It was something real inside me. I could form the words in my mind although it took some time to find the willpower. Acknowledging it in my mind made it more real. My mind went in all directions, and I felt many emotions: mainly scared, which paralyzed me. Even though I had acknowledged this enormous demon within me, it didn't mean that I was going to welcome it.

# Deep Dive: Acknowledgment

Once awareness is brought to our consciousness, acknowledgment is the next step. Acknowledgment is stating what is without any judgment or expectation. It is putting language to the actual awareness. Putting words to the awareness is like admitting the existence of something without guilt, shame or an agenda. This phase offers yourself permission to acknowledge what is and that it is presently a part of you or your situation.

# Magic Questions for Acknowledgment

What am I aware of?

What am I observing right now within/out me?

What is my greatest perceived struggle?

What is my current demon?

Where am I not showing up as ME?

# Let the Magic Happen!
## Journal Space for Personal Reflection

●

## BATTLEFIELD OF SCARS

TIRED AND RESTLESS, TOO NUMB TO TRANSMIT

CONSTANTLY FEELING MY WORRIES ARE LEGIT

GEARS KEEP GRINDING TO THE BEAT OF MY HEART

A CONSTANT POUNDING, MY MIND FALLS APART

TO THE MOUNTING PRESSURES AND STANDARDS SET

WHAT DO I BELIEVE AND WHAT SHOULD I FORGET

THE STRUGGLE IS REAL NO MATTER WHAT I FEEL

WHERE IS THE ANTIDOTE TO FIX ME AND HEAL

MY TOLERANCE TO PAIN IS A BATTLEFIELD OF SCARS

I FALL THROUGH THE CLOUDS REACHING FOR STARS

SYMBOLIC METAPHOR WITH AN ENDLESS POSSIBILITY

BRINGING SOME HOPE WHEN I'M SINKING IN REALITY

UNCERTAINTY IS LIFE WITH OPTIONS DEBATABLE

THE FREEDOM OF CHOICE AN UNWINDING VARIABLE

DISTORTION OF THE TRUTH BLOCKING MY VISION

AN UNWAVERING MOMENT WITH A CLEAR DECISION

A. LOVE

●

# TWO WORLDS COLLIDE

INSIDE I AM SCARED OF SHOWING THE REAL ME

REMOVING THE FAÇADE SO EVERYONE CAN SEE

THAT NOTHING HAS CHANGED EXCEPT FALSE EXPECTATIONS

THE FEAR OF LOSING LOVED ONES PREVENTS CONVERSATIONS

DIVIDING THE OBSTACLES OF DECISIONS TO MAKE

FOREVER HONORING MYSELF OR LIVING WITH THE HEARTACHE

I'LL DREAM OF THE DAY MY TWO WORLDS COLLIDE

WITH LOVE AS MY JOURNEY AND PEACE AS MY GUIDE

A. LOVE

# Phase III
# Allowance

Grams,

My mother continually says, "You always have options." As I was cruising on the highway in my truck on a road trip through Colorado, I began to look at my options moving forward. I can still see the rolling hills and feel the breeze on my arm extended out of the window. The sun was shining and the sky was clear. My mind, on the other hand, was clouded with thoughts.

I had to choose to either allow this demon to surface and face it, or keep it suppressed in the deepest crevices of my being with its continual whispers.

The other option was not having to deal with any of it: avoiding risking hardship, ache and rejection by ending my life. Was I ready to potentially be rejected or judged by the very people in my life who have always said their love was unconditional?

Grams, you are the epitome of unconditional love, and I was still scared to tell you because of how that could change the way you felt about me. It could have reshaped the entire fabric from which our relationship was woven. The realization of this demon felt like the weight of the world and appeared as a large screen on my mind. It naturally felt safer to stay in a secret and show only a version of myself than to risk the changes that could have affected our relationship.

Did I want to create the space of allowance to come face-to-face with this demon? Did I have enough strength and courage? Did I really want to enter into this struggle of finding peace within me, working through the shame of what this would bring up of "right" and "wrong" from two decades of conditioning by family, friends and society? This demon truly would change everything. I sensed that if I truly wanted a good life, I had no choice but to face it. I just had to muster up the courage to do so. The demon was living in the dark crevices of the caves within me, and it was time to own it before it grew too big and owned me.

It didn't take much time to find the answer because at my core, I knew that ending my life wasn't truly an option. Even though I flirted with death, I never danced with it. Ending my life and shortening my one existence would never be an option for me. I knew I had too much to offer the world with my gifts. My Soul knew that no demon was too big to face if I trusted the journey and had the right guidance along the way. It felt too big to handle, but any person is stronger than any struggle or any demon awaiting in the dark.

I allowed myself to save a seat at the table for my demon. I allowed myself to face the demon and for it to be recognized and truly seen and heard for the first time. Taking a leap into the uncertain, I invited the demon to dinner.

# Deep Dive: Allowance

Allowance means tolerating the given awareness and acknowledgment and offering it space to exist: a space without forced interaction.

Allow me to offer a story as an example: A stray cat lived on the porch of a house where five housemates were living. A few of them fell in love with this cat and committed themselves to feeding and taking care of it. Everyone in the house was aware of the cat, acknowledged it, and allowed it to live on the front porch after a house meeting was convened.

Two of the housemates wanted the cat to be able to live inside the house away from the dangers of the outdoors. However, that crossed over into the boundaries of acceptance. Most of the housemates allowed it to live on the front porch tolerating it but would not accept it inside.

Allowance gives the "*something*" space or tolerance to simply exist. Allowing the demon to be as is does not mean it is being accepted. This phase is powerful and liberating because it helps us surrender and let go.

The more something is ignored or resisted, the bigger it becomes. That *something* continues showing up in our lives just in different ways if not the same and is usually magnified. If we shove the demon back down or fight the demon, then it only gets louder and remains our perceived enemy. Until there is the courage to face it and work through it or with it, that perceived "ugly" will always be that shadow following your every move.

Instead of holding on or resisting something, there is an art of allowance. We must learn the art of surrendering and trusting something bigger than ourselves. There must live a hope within us that things will turn out well, that things can transform for the better.

We cannot always know when, why or how our demons will arise, but we can decide to be brave and step up to allow our demons to show up. Moments in life will always trigger us and bring up our baggage; these are the moments to celebrate and suit up!

Allowance gives us the time and space to figure out how to go about our approach with our inner demon we have acknowledged.

The demons within us exist and we do not have control over that. But how we go about greeting our demons is in our control. It is here that we must look at what is in our control, what is out of our control, and what we can influence. The beautiful thing we have control over is our approach and response to this guest renting space in our *house.*

We cannot force our inner demons to stay nor can we push them out. Sometimes, we must invite them to dinner to teach us all they have to offer. It is then that our demons can transform or vanish.

May we all find the courage to sit down to dinner and allow our inner demon(s) to join us as an opportunity to truly become liberated.

# Magic Questions for Allowance

What possibilities exist for me if I allow this?

What possibilities exist for me if I choose not to allow this?

How can I be more at peace with this part of me and all parts of me?

How can I choose to be a space that truly allows this demon to sit at the dinner table with me?

How can I change my relationship with this demon to give it space to exist (at least momentarily)?

How can I change my approach and response to the demon and its effects in my life to offer it allowance to exist (at least momentarily)?

What possible lessons might this demon have for me to learn if I open space of allowance for it?

# Let the Magic Happen!
## Journal Space for Personal Reflection

## LIFE'S LESSONS

EVERY DECISION WE MAKE IS CHOSEN WITHIN

WHICH WAY WE'LL GO AND WHERE TO BEGIN

OUR DESTINY IS BASED ON INTERNAL DIRECTION

BACKED BY LESSONS WITH OUR LIFE'S REFLECTION

HINDSIGHT WOULD CHANGE OUR FAITH'S INTERVENTION

PREVENTING GROWTH WITHOUT HONORABLE INTENTION

CONSIDER THE GOOD AND BAD COUNTING AS ONE

LEARN AND MOVE ON FROM WHAT'S ALREADY DONE

WE HAVE THE POWER TO CHANGE FROM THE PAST

TAKE AHOLD OF OUR FUTURE OWN WHAT WILL LAST

LIFE'S LESSONS ARE GREAT FOR THE MIND AND HEART

AN UNDENIABLE PATH WE OWN FROM THE START

A. LOVE

●

# DOUBLE VISION SINGLE VIEW

WITH THE ABILITY OF DOUBLE VISION WE SEEM TO USE
SINGLE VIEW

SEEING MANY DIFFERENT SIDES BUT TEND TO KEEP IT
SKEWED

IF WE'D OPEN OUR EYES TO THE COMPLETE BEAUTY AROUND

INSTEAD OF CHOOSING TO FOCUS ON PROBLEMS KEEPING US
DOWN

WE WOULD NOTICE THERE ARE MANY POSSIBILITIES TO
ATTAIN

BY PROCESSING AND ANALYZING SITUATIONS CAUSING
PAIN

BE AWARE OF YOUR HABITS BY REWRITING THEM WHEN
FOUND

LOOK PAST SITUATIONS THAT CONTINUE TO BE BOUND

BY CONSCIOUSLY REACTING AND CONTROLLING OUR
DOUBLE VISION

WITH LOVE AND ACCEPTANC BECOMING PART OF OUR
REVISION

A. LOVE

●

# Phase IV
# Acceptance

Grams,

For one year, I kept everything a secret. No one knew. I promised myself that I wouldn't say anything. I wore a mask of a straight man. When the topic of dating or relationships came up in conversation, I would just play along and either laugh or divert the conversation. Whether it was one of my family members trying to set me up with a *good girl* they knew or people asking about my relationship status, I would just give them the go-to answer: *Oh, it's not really my focus right now.* Or *I haven't found anyone that I'm interested in.*

And so it began: the journey of acceptance, which transpired step by step, one day at a time. I remember this process beginning with two books: *Radical Acceptance* by Tara Brach and *Daring Greatly* by Brené Brown. They were exactly what I needed at this time of my journey. These books helped me explore what it meant to be more authentic and vulnerable. They also guided me through shame and guilt. I found it difficult to accept myself for who I was, all parts of me. It wasn't easy to do.

I was miserable living a lie. I found myself combating between two worlds. I showed up as a version of myself that I wanted people to see. I was lying to them and to myself to play along with the intended script.

I remember kneeling in prayer in the living room of my apartment and going within for guidance and clarity. I was tapping into intuition and inspiration. It was then that I realized I needed to drop every single belief that I was ever taught by anyone else: society, friends and family. I had to intentionally reconstruct everything that I believed, but for me this time. I took the time to reconstruct my foundation and pillars instead of using borrowed bricks.

At this time, everything I believed was put on trial and questioned. It was time that I figured out what was true for me and what resonated for me, without the need for approval or acceptance of others. I was still trying to fit inside a box of approval of my parents, family members, friends, and society: *How could I make my father most proud? What would make my mother the happiest? What would my friends and brothers think? How would I fit into society?*

It was MY happiness's turn to get the lead in the play of my life. It was time to accept myself: radically accept myself.

For.

The.

First.

Time.

In.

My.

Life.

At this point, I knew I couldn't suppress the demon any longer now that I was fully conscious of it. I didn't want to get rid of it because I knew it was a part of me that wasn't inherently bad. I felt in my gut that it was leading me to become even greater and I had to trust that.

It was time to change my approach and accept this guest, and I wouldn't stop until the demon became my friend, until I learned all that it had to offer.

My happiness, my peace, my life was at a standstill unless I journeyed into acceptance of this part of me, this perceived ugly.

# Deep Dive: Acceptance

Demons come in all shapes and sizes. We never know when they will appear in our lives. From my experience, I believe that every demon arrives or shows up on time to take us on the journey that we need for further progression and growth. We choose some of our demons. We come with some of our demons. Some demons leave after they are given the time-of-day they need. Some remain and we choose how we live with them. The important thing is that we do not suppress them because they will only get louder and louder. A demon will always find its way out of the edges of our being.

To accept or not to accept? That is the question.

It is imperative that if the demon is a part of who you are at the core level, to find the courage to accept it and change your relationship with it as long as you have it around. Instead of fighting with this new dance partner, find a new rhythm and change your steps.

If the demon is an unhealthy or dangerous behavior, addiction or vice, then it is crucial to accept that it is in your life for a higher reason and can lead you to the greatest version of yourself. This does not mean that you have to accept it in the sense of giving into and letting it destroy your life. It becomes all about the approach of loving-kindness and mindfulness as you find a way that is best for you to resolve and consider all that the demon has to offer. It is about seeking all the resources that can aid you in channeling the perceived demon to best live with it or conquer it and even allow it to vanish.

Accepting something is the process of being at peace sitting with the demon without fighting it. This is usually one of the longest and most difficult steps along the journey: one that comes with negative thoughts, guilt, shame, and sometimes years of conditioning to unravel. Most inner demons will lead us to the inner wounded child that needs to be heard and liberated. Along with using all your tools and resources to aid you, this phase is also a good time to think of a person(s) in whom you can confide for additional support.

It is in the process and landscape of acceptance that turmoil transforms to peace, struggle to contentment, stress to relief, despair to hope.

Invite your demons to dinner and see what they have to teach you. From there, either they stay with you as a teacher/friend or they disappear after having been truly seen and heard.

# Magic Questions for Acceptance

What can I do that creates space to radically accept myself even with this demon and even if those close to me can't do the same?

What energy can I be to create compassion and openness that allows space for acceptance and love of this part of me/my life?

What narrative am I choosing to believe about the importance of the judgments of others?

Where have I agreed to shrink and define my infinite Self to this reality?

What else is possible to honor and accept all of who I am?

How can I find a different way of seeing *this* or being with *this* so I am at peace and not war?

Does this bring me to my more authentic and joyful self? If not, what can I change about it?

If I cannot accept this demon, how can I peacefully allow it to transform so that it benefits my life?

How can I conquer or transcend this demon?

In what ways does my approach with this demon/its message add to and/or diminish my life and me?

# Let the Magic Happen!
## Journal Space for Personal Reflection

# EVER WONDER

EVER WONDER HOW YOU TELL SOMEONE
WHAT YOU FEEL INSIDE
TO OPEN UP AND EXPRESS ONESELF
WITHOUT WANTING TO HIDE

EVER WONDER HOW THE WORDS WILL SOUND
AND MAYBE COME ACROSS
HOPING TO BE UNDERSTOOD
WITHOUT GETTING LOST

EVER WONDER WHY PEOPLE JUDGE
WITHOUT KNOWING MORE
ONLY SEEING WHAT THEY WANT
COMPLETELY BEING IGNORED

EVER WONDER WHAT'S IN-STORE
FOR THE FUTURE YOU BEHOLD
HOPING FOR THE BEST
WITHOUT BEING TOLD

BELIEVING IN YOURSELF
AND HOLDING ON TO DREAMS
REACHING OUT FOR SOMEONE
WHO SURPASSES ALL THESE THINGS

A. LOVE

## CLOSED OFF

WHY IN A WORLD FULL OF MANY, DO I FEEL ALONE

HIDING MY EMOTIONS, CAREFULLY NOT SHOWN

WHY DO I CHOOSE, TO CLOSE MYSELF INSIDE

INSTEAD OF REACHING, FOR SOMEONE TO GUIDE

WHY DO I LET MYSELF, COMPLETELY GO NUMB

RELIVING DIFFERENT EVENTS, UNTIL I FEEL DUMB

WHY DOES MY PRIDE, DILIGENTLY HOLD BACK TEARS

REVOLVING AROUND STRESS, STACKED UP BY FEARS

WHY DO I BELIEVE, THE INSULTS THROWN MY WAY

AND THEN DISREGARD, COMPLIMENTS LIKE HEARSAY

WHY DO I FEEL, THE PERSISTENT NEED TO KNOW

WHEN THE DIFINITIVE REALITY, IS BETTER TO LET GO

WHY DO I REACT, TO HEARTACHES OF THE PAST

INSTEAD OF LEARNING, AND PUSHING TO SURPASS

WHY IS THE QUESTION, I ASK MYSELF EACH DAY

PUSHING PEOPLE AWAY, SECRETLEY WANTING TO STAY

WHY DO I ANALYZE, JUST STEP BACK AND FORSAKE

BE COMPASSIONATE, KNOW LIFE IS WHAT YOU MAKE

A. LOVE

# Phase V
# Alignment

Grams,

As my self-acceptance expanded, things in my life began shifting and realigning. I took a look at my beliefs, rules and life-structure and began to evaluate where I needed to align myself and life to be completely true to me.

I began with my foundation. From a very young age, I believed there was a God, and that has been my foundation since I was young: something I could lean on. A spiritual practice was always important to me throughout my life. I never really fit into any one box of ideas or beliefs. I have always had a firm faith, but it has never been a closed faith. This was a blessing for me because I needed the gates of my open faith to broaden more than it ever had before. This was no time to abandon my spiritual path; it was time to re-evaluate and realign my practice to honor who I really was.

I even had to momentarily drop the belief that there was a God in order to reconstruct *my* beliefs, *my* pillars, *my* spiritual structure, *my* practice. Completely collapsed and ready for construction, I rebuilt my belief system, rules and life structure, brick by brick. The leftover bricks were ones that no longer resonated with me: these were bricks I held onto for approval, protection, validation and because of old conditioning. Now it was time to accept myself and no longer fear others' acceptance of me.

I changed how I attended worship services, and I visited a variety of traditions and services depending on where I felt pulled by my intuition. I started to honor my yearning to connect with Mother Earth by being in nature more. I began meditating/chanting more often with traditions and communities in which I resonated. Instead of fighting or hiding my more feminine qualities, I embraced them, which in turn increased my confidence and my groundedness in my masculinity. It felt liberating to live more of my truth.

I was finally getting closer to living a life that was stamped with the approval of ME. This was the first time in my life I had the courage to reorganize and realign everything to truly resonate with who I was.

It's funny how Life offers us what we need in order to go deeper into creating ourselves. Universe always knows the next step, the next turn. I felt more confident in my identity, masculinity and path.

~~~

Curiosity filled me after some time leading me to wonder if I was capable of having a successful and happy relationship with a woman, especially after all of this inner work. What would it feel like now that I was more at peace and confident with myself?

One day, as I was walking downtown, I felt inclined to talk to this beautiful Latina. We hit it off and slowly built a connection and a fun relationship and ended up dating for a few months. It was great. I was full-heartedly into her, and it felt like any prior inner conflict was resolved. But after three months, my attraction could not be sustained and my attraction and attention towards men returned.

I stayed in the relationship long enough to know how unhappy I was by remaining in it. I eventually broke up with her. It was time to finally accept that I might never date a woman again. I needed to continue in my journey of self-acceptance and alignment. This meant taking a step into the unknown even more. This meant considering dating men for the first time. Deep down I also knew it was time to begin telling my family.

~~~

The isolation I felt from my family was at an all-time high due to it still being a kept secret. They didn't know the true me. I still remember the day we all gathered together and I felt so alone: I felt as if I no longer fit into their world. I was a visitor from the outside.

Up to this point of the journey, I had refused to allow anyone to know about this inner demon of mine. I was too scared. Consequently, the more I kept it a secret, the bigger it became; I realized that I needed to share it with someone, and it had to begin with family. It wasn't healthy to keep it all inside and navigate it all on my own.

Even though I knew I had people who cared about me and wouldn't truly care about my sexual orientation, my fear was always too big to allow myself to open my mouth. I projected my fear onto the situation, which kept me paralyzed for so long. I cared too much of others' opinions. I found myself capable of loving others unconditionally, but I couldn't find myself capable of trusting that others would do the same.

It was time to find the support and allow this part of me to be known. Paradoxically at the same time however, I was prepared and armed to say goodbye to anyone in my life who was not capable of accepting me.

I decided that if someone wasn't going to support me in this, I didn't want them around in my life anymore, which made me prepared to say my goodbyes. This was one of the most difficult heart-walls I had to put up in defense to potential rejection.

And so it was Grams, a large part of this acceptance and clearing the shame and guilt was telling someone. After too long of being with this secret, I finally found the courage to open my mouth and tell the first person. I knew that for me, I needed that person to be in my nuclear family.

The first person I decided to tell was my twin brother. I still remember we were sitting outside, and I was so terrified to tell him. After some time conversing, I finally said the words aloud, and I felt like I was having an out-of-body experience. My heart was beating; I was shaking; my face was flushed; I couldn't think or see straight. He was so gentle with me acknowledging what I had said and navigating it with questions. We had a good conversation. That was one of the greatest gifts he could have offered me in that moment.

Next, I decided to tell my father. We were on a trip in Florida as our tradition had it. We were both sitting facing each other on the beach. I began shaking as we talked, wanting so badly for the words to come out, but they never did. I couldn't speak them in front of him. I dropped hints, and he finally asked me. He helped me come out to him, and I'm so grateful he did. Beautifully enough, he asked questions and processed it with me gently. I know how scary this realization must have been for him. He wasn't super surprised having often wondered over the years. Maybe this cushioned the landing for him.

At that point, my father ended up telling my stepmother. I waited until our next family gathering to tell her in person. As a counselor, she was naturally inquisitive, open and supportive. Another tender mercy.

During that same time, space opened up for my sister-in-law and I to talk and connect: I felt like there was no better time than in that moment to share the secret. I ended up telling her and she was surprisingly very gentle and supportive. She told me that she couldn't even imagine what I was going through. She encouraged me to tell my older brother and helped make time to do that. As she put my nephews to bed that night, my older brother and I talked for awhile and he told me that we never know why we are the way we are, but there's always a reason and purpose. I felt supported and loved even though I knew neither of them agreed with it. They were and still are the ultimate example of unconditional love and non-judgment.

The secret was out. Finally! It was as if a boulder lifted from my heart and lungs and I could take a deep breath again feeling lighter. I had finally told most of my family--everyone but my mother: she would be visiting within the month, and I would tell her then. Some people come out to their friends first; some to a trusted family member outside of the home; some come out to their family by a mass email; by someone else spreading the news by text or call: I needed to come out face-to-face, one-on-one.

A few weeks later my mother came into town and the last couple of nights she was in town, she ended up staying with me in my apartment. It was evening time, and we were in my living room when I decided to tell her. It took a moment for me to get it out. She sensed something was up as she always does with me. She was relieved that I had finally told her what was going on; she was supportive and inquisitive. There wasn't even a pause in her response as if all was fine.

What a difference it made for me to tell my nuclear family: not only a difference within me, but a difference in my relationship with them.

It wasn't easy for anyone to really grasp and it took some time and still is taking time for it to fully integrate with my family. My father recommended that I go to therapy to see if I could go deeper and figure things out. I reluctantly decided to give it a try and although it did help me focus on patterns I needed to shift to have healthier relationships in general, it didn't feel right. So after a few sessions, I called it quits. With the undercurrent of feeling like I was trying to be fixed, I knew deep down there was nothing to fix or get rid of. It's exhausting trying to fix something that isn't broken.

I needed to nurture this new friend who at times still felt like the old demon. My journey continued forward as did my family's, trying to process everything. It was only fair to give them time and honor their journey of understanding and tolerance.

I appreciated that my family all embraced me in their own way during my journey as they had the choice to reject me. There are so many who are kicked out of their families: something I was prepared for but never had to venture through. No matter the severity of the storm, it will always run out of rain, eventually!

~~~

There is a time in this process that I began to grieve the loss of my old life and all that it offered. Part of the phase of acceptance consisted of allowing myself to grieve what would never be the same again in order to move forward in my life and where I knew Universe was guiding me.

Grams, up to this time, my sexual orientation felt like the biggest and loudest part of me. It had become my entire world even though it was simply one small part of me just like with any other characteristic. Because it was going against all conditioning and had not been truly explored, it had taken up the entire stage of my mind for so long. That was finally beginning to change!

I found myself spending my time with like-minded people. With more alignment came deeper acceptance. In turn, I felt a greater happiness and congruency in my life.

# Deep Dive: Alignment

Alignment is another phase that naturally occurs as we continue choosing to face our once-perceived demons. It is all about creating congruency in your life. This is the phase where change really starts happening. Aspects of your identity and life shift, shed, and realign to resonate with the new accepted you and your life. When this takes place, it creates space to truly live authentically and tap into the happiness that you have withheld from yourself for so long.

This is the space and time to re-examine all beliefs, structures, narratives, goals and conditionings to truly have your life support this authentic you.

You must:

1. Question everything and be okay living in the question as some answers and new revelations take time.

2. Look with a different perspective

3. Surround yourself with what and who nurture you most

4. Embrace the mantra *I choose me!*

5. Create and upgrade new thoughts, habits, tools, people, places, resources, programs, routines etc. that best uplift you into living your true authentic Self.

Alignment is all about making sure that everything is in line with who you truly are. No more versions of yourself:

just your whole self. Whatever no longer nurtures you, erase it from your narrative. Write into your story only what embraces who you are wholeheartedly with no reservations.

Navigating this new landscape might feel different at first and it may not always be easy. The once-perceived demon may even continue to be loud. But there is peace and a new rhythm in which you may dance--maybe even a larger floor on which to dance. It is in the alignment to our higher Self that authenticity can sprout and gratitude can blossom.

# Magic Questions for Alignment

What space can I be to allow room for new structures and paradigms to come flowing into my life that support my true Self?

What other possibilities exist to create the most supportive life for me that I am not yet recognizing?

Where am I not living for me but for someone or something else? How can I change that in order to choose me?

Where am I still a version of myself and not my whole self?

What changes do I need to make to allow my authentic self to show up?

What other realities are possible to birth the life that will best support me to allow myself to use my gifts to contribute to the world?

What or who do I need to shed from my life to allow the most congruency and potency of me to manifest?

How can I nurture me even more than I am already doing?

How can I receive more from Universe and all that She has to offer?

# Let the Magic Happen!
## Journal Space for Personal Reflection

# FAMILY

THERE ARE PEOPLE IN YOUR LIFE THAT YOU GRAVITATE TO

WHO HAVE KNOWN YOU FOR YEARS OR MAYBE JUST A FEW

GUIDING AND DIRECTING THROUGH LESSONS THEY
LEARNED

SHOWING YOU ENDURANCE EVEN IF YOU'VE BEEN BURNED

THEIR LOVE AND DEVOTION FULFILLS YOUR INNER NEED

CREATING ACCEPTANCE TO OVERCOME AND SUCCEED

YOUR ULTIMATE FAMILY YOU CHOOSE TO SURROUND

NOT ALWAYS BY BLOOD, BUT WHO YOU LOVE TO BE AROUND

THEY ARE LOYAL TO YOU THROUGH THE THICK AND THIN

STANDING RIGHT BY YOUR SIDE, KNOWING WHERE TO BEGIN

THEY FREELY GIVE ADVICE TO SHOW THAT THEY CARE

OFFERING COMPASSION TO COMFORT YOU AND SHARE

ENDLESS SUPPORT BUILDING YOUR CHARACTER STRONG

FOREVER THANKFUL IN KNOWING THAT WE ALL BELONG

A. LOVE

# CLEANSING

GETTING RID OF THOSE THAT WEIGH YOU DOWN

CAUSING YOU GRIEF WHEN THEY'RE AROUND

DIMMING THE LIGHT BURNING OUT YOUR FLAME

DIMINISHING THE SPARK LOWERING YOUR AIM

START CLEANSING YOUR TIME AND YOUR SPACE

MOTIVATE YOUR HEART FIND A COMMONPLACE

UNDERSTAND YOUR VALUE THAT'S KEPT WITHIN

SHINING INSIDE WHERE IT HAS ALWAYS BEEN

YOU CAN ACCOMPLISH ANYTHING YOU BELIEVE

PEACE, LOVE, AND WORTH WAITING TO RETRIEVE

A. LOVE

# Phase VI
# Appreciation

Grams,

A once-hated demon can slowly become a gift greatly cherished with some loving-kindness, compassion and mindfulness. Some of the best gifts in life are the ones that come with the most struggle.

I would never ask my demons upon anyone else. They are personal, and they are stubborn. They are also specific to me and what my soul needs for growth and progress. The process has been and continues to be painful and difficult at times, but it's worth it.

Throughout this process, a beam of gratitude for the demon began to shine. I started smiling when thinking of my once-before demon, now friend. I started seeing the good that was coming from *the bad*. I started feeling appreciation and even admiration for this upgraded me that came from my *demon*.

Thanks to my once-perceived demon, I was pushed to go within and find myself, recreate myself; I was inspired to question and challenge all the rules I had set up about life and my identity; I was able to embrace myself in ways I never would have before to truly accept and love myself; I realized that the secret to happiness is living my life authentically and being 100% unapologetically me without a care of the judgmental darts forever thrown by others; I became closer with my Creator; I found the ability to receive and give love in an intimate relationship which I hadn't fully experienced yet in my lifetime.

A journey towards a greater self-love takes time and nourishment: someone cannot eat a salad once and say they are healthy for the rest of their lives. It takes the next right thing again and again. That goes for the journey of true living as well. Would I want to go through all of this again? No. But I sure am grateful that Life took me on this journey with Universe having my back.

# Deep Dive: Appreciation

Finding a different perspective and feeling even a sliver of gratitude shows that the relationship between you and the once-perceived demon has changed to create more peace, joy and love. There is healing and unity truly taking place for solid, enduring change.

There is a reason each individual is the way he/she is. Humans want to understand the why, but sometimes it does not always appear. There is always something from which to learn or grow. Our greatest perceived wounds can transform into our greatest gifts. It is about the "gift" that takes the soul on a journey: sometimes the most valuable journey of a lifetime.

Usually appreciation or admiration is felt when the heaviness of the storm has passed; the clouds clear up and new clarity is born. And of course, it is in the greatest struggle where the greatest growth happens. Hopefully, the journey leads one to a state of gratitude and love for the whole self: the once-upon-a-time demon is now something for which to be thankful.

The butterfly cannot survive without the struggle of coming out of its chrysalis. The chick cannot survive without the struggle of hatching from the shell of its egg. They would simply die if the struggle was taken from them. We cannot afford to not face the demons that call us. Appreciation is the portal to true opportunity and transformation because it is too easy to see the negative and feel the bitterness.

We never know the bigger reason for our demons. We never know where they will lead us. We only have a portion of the tapestry of the canvas of life. All we can do is understand for ourselves what the truth is that resonates most with our Soul and follow that truth, hoping that it only burns brighter and brighter along the way. If it leads to happiness and peace, I say keep on that path. If it leads to love and growth, I say keep moving forward. If you get to be the authentic you with all your gifts, I say what a beautiful journey!

# Magic Questions for Appreciation

What gifts can come/have come from this inner demon/journey?

How am I stronger and more authentic from this inner demon/journey?

Where is there more peace and vitality in my life now with this different relationship with this part of me?

Where can I turn perceived struggles/lows into new possibilities for growth and opportunity?

What lessons have I learned?

What would my future-self tell my present-self right now concerning my life, my path, and my approach to facing this inner demon?

What am I grateful for about my life and myself?

# Let the Magic Happen!
## Journal Space for Personal Reflection

# FROZEN

TIME FROZEN STILL MAKES EVERYTHING APPEAR

FREE AS A BIRD, PEACEFUL AND CLEAR

CLOUDED THOUGHTS AND UNKNOWN DECISIONS

KEEP US FROM, SOME OF OUR VISIONS

TRYING TO DECIDE THE STEPS TO TAKE

TO RISE ABOVE, LIVE AND CREATE

DRIVING WITH COURAGE, HOLDING ON TIGHT

ACCOMPLISHING WHAT WE HAVE SET IN SIGHT

PASSION DETERMINES SUCCESS IN OUR LIFE

WHEN WE CAN LOOK PAST ALL THE STRIFE

A. LOVE

## PERFECTLY IMPERFECT

EVERYONE IN THIS WORLD, IS PERFECTLY IMPERFECT

STARTING WITH THE DEFINITION, WE TRY TO INTERCEPT

BECAUSE NO ONE SHOULD, CONFORM TO A SYMBOL

IDEOLOGY REVOLVING, DEMANDING YOU RESEMBLE

A SPECIFIC LEVEL, TO WHICH WE MUST ACHIEVE

WHEN WE ARE THE ONES, THAT DECIDE TO BELIEVE

A CERTAIN PATH, DRIVING TOWARDS DETERMINATION

CONSTRUCT AND EVOLVE, REINVENT YOUR MOTIVATION

FULFILL YOUR JOURNEY, CEMENTED WITH CHARACTER

REWRITING YOUR FUTURE, BECOMING YOUR NARRATOR

NEVER TRY TO BLEND, STAND OUT FROM THE CROWD

STAY TRUE TO YOURSELF, YOU WILL FOREVER BE PROUD

THERE WILL ALWAYS BE FLAWS, THAT'S A GUARANTEE

LIVE LIFE TO THE FULLEST, EVENTUALLY BE CAREFREE

LOVE HEALS ALL WOUNDS, AND UPLIFTS OUR SOULS

HELPING US FORGIVE AND TO CONQUER OUR GOALS

A. LOVE

# Phase VII
# Authenticity


Grams,

You know how I love to travel and am always on the move! Well, at this time of my life, my soul was calling me to go take a year to travel and teach abroad, which I had always wanted to do. But I also knew that I had to get things in order. For my last year before going abroad, I started preparing and becoming a minimalist. To anchor myself into my authenticity, I knew I needed to leave the bounds of family ties and step into my soul's yearning for a cultural adventure. It would be my time to ground myself in who I was while at the same time spread my wings.

I ended up donating and getting rid of almost everything I owned except for two backpacks worth of belongings, which were going with me abroad to a land that had called me: Israel/Palestine. My intention was to teach abroad somewhere in Southeast Asia, but I was called elsewhere. I believe that Universe always has the next step ready for us when we are ready to step forward.

Many people leave their surroundings in hopes to escape their demons. But they come with us because they are a part of us. No matter where we are, there we are. In other words, no matter where we go, we bring all that we are, including our demons, with us. Even though I was following a long-time soul calling, I had to make sure I wasn't leaving to escape my demon. With intuition and inspiration, I knew that it was the right timing for this chapter of my life. It was time to expand my horizon and follow my heart and soul's yearning.

Before taking off and beginning my new journey away from the four-corner states, I ended up telling the first person outside of my nuclear family about my sexual orientation: a close colleague and friend from the school where I first taught. She was super supportive.

~~~

With just two backpacks, I landed in Israel the evening of my thirtieth birthday. I remember stepping into the warm Mediterranean Sea with the sunset and moon above me: all new sounds, smells, sights. I felt at peace; I knew I was right where I needed to be.

Until well into my time here, I didn't know why I was called to teach in this sacred land; however, I knew it would change me for the better. Everyone I met there helped me grow and see life in new ways. It was a blessed time to experience all that this land, people and culture had to offer. I was living who I was born to be and embracing the opportunities Life offered me. Everything and everyone I met were divinely orchestrated, along with the timing of it all.

Everything created more space for my authentic self to shine and be truly anchored. I was on fire and felt solid about who I was and my life's direction.

~~~

Upon my return from this life changing experience, I reintegrated back in the beautiful vortex of Sedona, Arizona. Being gone for a year along with jetlag requires a solid time period to truly transition. I rooted myself in my new intention of being and a sense of confidence in honoring my true self, no matter the cost.

When the topic came up naturally and genuinely in a conversation, I was able to talk about my sexual orientation as if it was just another part of me as was me being a teacher or loving the outdoors. What was once paralyzing to put into words was now no big deal to share: coming out to family members, friends and new acquaintances. Nothing had changed about my situation--I changed. I came from a place of more acceptance and self-love, and that makes all the difference.

People will always judge no matter what. I have had five plus years to process this part of me. It is now time for others to process as they need. I am no longer attached to others' reactions or judgments because I am living my truth.

I returned from Israel with such groundedness and certainty and in return, received all kinds of responses:

*"Really? You are? Wait, are you joking? Well, I always wondered. So tell me more about that."*

*"Okay."*

*"I don't care and I don't not care. You are you and that aspect of you doesn't matter to me."*

*"We support you. We love you. You and your partner are always welcome into our home."*

*"I can't have you around our children. I don't want them to think that it's okay to be gay since their cool uncle is."*

*"I am no longer praying for your gay to go away. I am now praying for your happiness."*

*"Heck man, as long as you don't hit on me, we're good."*

*"It doesn't change anything."*

*"Thank you so much for telling me."*

Some conversations were intense and difficult and others were energizing and relaxed. There was no going back now. I made the intention to stay true to my heart, to stay true to me because the cost of me not doing so would be detrimental.

# Deep Dive: Authenticity

Being authentic means being real and true to yourself: no masks. To live authentically is a journey. There are always more and new ways to be truer to ourselves. There will be times in our lives where we simply forget or get busy and go back three steps from which we came. There will be relationships that disorient us. There will be trials that exhaust us. It is simply about always coming back to our true selves, our higher Selves: to all of who we are.

Often, we show versions of ourselves to different people depending on their role and projected agenda/judgments. We often seek approval, feelings of importance and love from others by negating parts of who we are to fit in. The secret to happiness is finding contentment in being your authentic self because that is when you share your gifts with the world most. Too often, we play small so that we do not stand out or so that others will accept us. We want others to be happy over our own happiness.

I think Shakespeare had it right when he wrote in one of his greatest plays, *Hamlet,* "This above all: to thine own self be true." Happiness shines with the fewer masks and versions of ourselves we wear. Here in the space of authenticity there are no versions of oneself: you show up 100% unapologetically you. Obviously, different situations call for different aspects of you to shine more than other aspects but you are still *you*--not trying to be or act like something/one you are not.

Being authentic means recognizing all parts as you and owning that *you* are the greatest gift to the world. *You* are and have something that no one else in the world has to offer; there is no other *you*.

When you live more of *you*, Universe responds by opening doors for opportunity and possibility. Taking these courageous actions communicate to Universe you are ready for the beauty on the horizon that is all yours and always has been. It is all about inner integration of unapologetic authenticity.

People are not inspired by a flower that has not yet bloomed. They wait. People take in the beauty of a flower when it is at its full bloom. Authenticity is our blossoming that truly inspires the world around us.

# Magic Questions for Authenticity

How can I be even more of the amazing self I am?

What aspects of my life are still not authentically me?

What space can I be to receive more authenticity?

In what ways can I be gentler with myself?

Where can I give myself more credit than I am currently offering?

In what areas of my life am I being true to myself?

In what areas of my life am I not being true to myself?

What are the different versions of myself currently?

Can I drop one or two of them to be truer to me?

Where am I not truly showing up as 100% unapologetically me?

What possibilities exist for me to reach that 100%?

# Let the Magic Happen!
## Journal Space for Personal Reflection

# BEST SHOT

POSITIVITY IN THIS LIFE IS THE KEY TO SUCCESS

WHAT YOU DREAM OF AND WHAT YOU POSSESS

THE QUALITIES AND TRAITS TO INSPIRE MORE

IDEAS AND CREATIVITY DEEP IN YOUR CORE

ACHIEVE YOUR GOALS WITH INCREASED UNITY

PASSIONATELY EMBRACE EVERY OPPORTUNITY

TAKE YOUR BEST SHOT AT LIVING YOUR DREAM

BY CARRYING OUT YOUR WILDEST SCHEME

THERE'S ONLY ONE LIFE SO MAKE IT COUNT

CLEAR YOUR HEAD GET RID OF YOUR DOUBT

THERE IS NOTHING STANDING IN YOUR WAY

EXCEPT YOUR MOTIVATION STUCK ON DELAY

A. LOVE

●

# INTENTIONS

ALONG THIS JOURNEY THROUGH THIS THING CALLED LIFE

WE'LL UNFORTUNATELY CREATE A FAIR SHARE OF STRIFE

MANY GOOD INTENTIONS TURNING FOR THE WORSE

COMMENTS TWISTED FOREVER WISHING TO REVERSE

NEVER LET A MISTAKE CHALLENGE YOUR POTENTIAL

OVERCOME HEARTACHE WITH FORGIVENESS INFLUENTIAL

FOCUS ON THE FUTURE OF WHERE YOU WANT TO BE

WITH LOVE AND ACCEPTANCE SETTING YOU FREE

A. LOVE

●

# Phase VIII
# Amplification

Grams,

I've waited so long to share my story with you. It's been quite the journey. And it doesn't end. I march forth as life unfolds, evolves and continually recalibrates.

The perceived demon ended up becoming one of my greatest friends, guides and teachers. With it, I would never have looked this deeply within myself to find and intentionally craft my authentic self and the life I was meant to live.

Now, as my true, happy and authentic self, my life is filled with self-love and alignment. I am grateful for this part of me. Now that congruency exists in my life, I am able to amplify my potency; I am able to amplify my gifts and share them with the world around me.

~~~

I had a big decision to make upon returning to the United States: where would I call my new home? After feeling into all of my options, Atlanta, Georgia called to me the loudest. And it was there that I felt a meaningful relationship and shift in my career path awaiting me, along with a beautiful part of Mother Earth to explore!

I was ready to get out of my comfort zone to expand my skill set and ability to make a difference. I began my journey in starting my own business to work in more fulfilling ways to enhance the lives of others along with a continued teaching career. I also furthered my education, which had been a desire for some time.

I entered into a relationship with a man where, for the first time, I was truly able to give and receive love, venturing into the depth and edges of my heart never truly explored to such a degree.

There came a time where I had to consciously choose to no longer squelch myself to make others happy or comfortable. What a beautiful life when I am living my potential and amplifying my gifts and potency of who I am. I believe Universe opens up the way to a more effortless life when we live our true selves and journey towards a greater self-love guided by these eight A's of greater living.

It's not about me coming out as gay. It's about me coming out to the whole world as ME, sharing my talents and being myself without holding back.

~~~~

Well, like I told you Grams, I had so much to share: a journey that has changed and enhanced my life immensely. I am so grateful that I finally had the chance to share it with you.

I cannot wait … *when I see you again.*

# Deep Dive: Amplification

Play BIG! It is time to get louder and make a positive difference in the world around you.

Marianne Williamson said it the best when she stated, "Our deepest fear is not that we are inadequate. Our deepest fear is that we are powerful beyond measure."

Amplification is the space in which you get to spread your wings and soar: create; live big; open up; share your gifts; pursue your dreams; do not hold back; connect with people; drop the labels; be *all* you; feel alive and be on fire!

This is where you are most authentic and find your greatest gifts you were born to emanate. And Universe responds to this frequency of being.

In this space, you whole-heartedly and completely love yourself and see that all the ingredients that make you who you are, ugly and beautiful, create the perfect recipe for you to grow, learn and become your best self.

It is in the darkness that we truly call on our inner light to shine brighter. It is in the struggle that we are stretched enough with pain and discomfort to change and grow. Without the friction, there would be no fire. Without the compression, there would be no diamond.

# Magic Questions for Amplification

What matters most to me?

What passions and life callings am I not yet heeding?
How can I make them manifest?

In what ways can I invite vulnerability more into my life to grow?

How can I show up and step up with all I have to offer?

What possibilities exist to amplify my gifts and all parts of me?

Where can I play even BIGGER in the game of life?

How can I get out of my own way and allow Universe and Life to bring me the next adventure/lesson/gift?

What positive affirmations do I need to write down and hear myself say each day to create a more expansive inner narrative?

Where can I let go of *self* and be more of <u>*Self*</u>?

# Let the Magic Happen!
## Journal Space for Personal Reflection

# Epilogue

## *From the Caves: Another Demon Awakens*

### ~ Anxiety ~

The burning pain hit again, every day at the same time. The pain wasn't going away nor was it going to allow me to ignore it. I was fully aware that something wasn't right. I was sixteen years old at the time.

No matter what I did, nothing helped. I went to several health care practitioners only to find out that I had stomach ulcers induced from years of anxiety. I acknowledged the situation and all I had to face.

*How do I get rid of the ulcers? The anxiety?*

I believed that I had no choice but to face the demon with one aim: demolish it. The burning would get so bad making me want to vomit. Food was the only thing that seemed to diminish some of the fire burning in the pit of my stomach. At least I found something to help, but I knew that wasn't getting to the root of the problem: the demon.

What was it trying to tell me?

It would be easy to get a pill for this; there were many, but I was determined to dominate this naturally and at the core.

Through the process, I finally realized I needed to invite this demon to dinner and learn what it had to teach me. I changed my relationship with it. Instead of fighting my anxiety and getting annoyed by it, I learned to live with my anxiety as a gift of guidance. I found ways to calm it down (using breath, mind-reframing, and other tools) so I could still accomplish my goals and participate in challenging activities outside of my comfort zone. Anxiety has been my gift of telling me when I am not being true to mySelf or where I am stuck in my life and need to clear mental/emotional baggage. My anxiety is my compass of alignment for the life that brings the most joy. It has helped me slow down and approach life more intentionally.

Instead of fighting my anxiety every day, I greet it. And from there, we transform together.


~ Insecurities and Fears ~

Just when I thought I had faced a loud inner demon and there couldn't be anymore, I entered into a relationship, which shook the caves and awakened my inner demons of fear, insecurities and limiting beliefs. It unlocked emotional childhood scars forgotten in the edges of the unconscious. The relationship was the portal from which to reveal another level of going within myself to truly become unbound, truly free.



Courage is about showing up day-in and day-out because in this life we get one shot, one chance to accept the challenge. So my advice is...

Invite the Demon to Dinner.

And maybe,
    just maybe,
        you'll see that your inner demon
            is really your inner wisdom.

# ABOUT THE AUTHOR

Jason Miller is a Colorado native. After working extensively in teen mentoring and living in the Middle East, he returned to the United States where he currently resides in Atlanta, Georgia. He is an educator in public schools, a certified life coach and Neuro-Linguistic Programming practitioner, and a mentor and mediator amongst diverse young adults and families. Jason works to promote equity for all marginalized people believing in humanKINDness.

**Living On Fire, LLC.**
**TheLoveUGive.net**

CPSIA information can be obtained
at www.ICGtesting.com
Printed in the USA
BVHW041223280920
589766BV00012B/1373